Geography Starts

DESERTS

Andy Owen
and
Miranda Ashwell

Heinemann Interactive Library
Des Plaines, Illinois

© 1998 Reed Educational & Professional Publishing
Published by Heinemann Interactive Library,
an imprint of Reed Educational & Professional Publishing,
Chicago, IL

Customer Service 888-454-2279

Visit our website at www.heinemannlibrary.com

Designed by Susan Clarke
Illustrations by Oxford Illustrators (maps pp.23, 25, 27)
Printed in China by WKT Company Limited

09 08 07
10 9 8 7 6 5

Library of Congress Cataloging-in-Publication Data
Owen, Andy, 1961-
    Deserts / Andy Owen and Miranda Ashwell.
        p.   cm. — (Geography starts)
    Includes bibliographical references and index.
    Summary: An introduction to the deserts of the world and the
unique characteristics of their environment.
        ISBN 1-57572-605-X (lib. bdg.)   ISBN 1-58810-970-4 (pbk. bdg.)
        ISBN 978-1-57572-605-2 (HC)   ISBN 978-1-58810-970-5 (pbk)

        1. Deserts—Juvenile literature.   [1. Deserts.]   I. Ashwell,
Miranda, 1957- . II. Title.   III. Series: Owen, Andy, 1961-
Geography starts.
GB12..094   1998
551.41'5—dc21   97-34421
                                                                                  CIP
                                                                                  AC

Acknowledgments
The publishers would like to thank the following for permission to reproduce photographs:
Barnaby's Picture Library, p. 21; Bill Bachman, pp. 22, 24, 26; Bruce Coleman Ltd, p. 13 (Gerald Cubitt), p. 7 (Mr Jules
Cowan), p. 14 (David Hughes), p. 9 (John Murray); FLPA, p. 5 (W. Wisniewski), p. 10 (Martin Withers); Magnum/Steve
McCurry, p. 19; Oxford Scientific Films, p. 11 (Marty Cordano), p. 4 (Stan Osolinski); Planet Earth, p. 29, pp. 16, 18
(Thomas Dressler), p. 6 (John Evans), p. 12 (Peter Stephenson), p. 17 (Ronald Rogott); Tony Stone, p. 15 (Frank
Heroldt), p. 28 (Duncan Wherrett)

Cover photograph: Oxford Scientific Films/Stan Osolinski

Our thanks to Betty Root for her comments in the preparation of this book.

Every effort has been made to contact copyright holders of any material reproduced in this book. Any omissions will
be rectified in subsequent printings if notice is given to the publisher.

Some words are shown in bold, **like this**. You can find
out what they mean by looking in the glossary.

Contents

Deserts are Dry

All deserts are dry places. It may not rain for months or years.

This desert is sandy.

This desert is rocky.

Most deserts are sandy or rocky places. Only special plants and animals can live where it is so dry.

Flat and Hilly Deserts

Some deserts are flat so you can see a very long way. Traveling across deserts can be difficult because there are few roads.

The Sahara Desert in Africa takes days to cross.

These desert mountains have flat tops.

Many deserts have hills and mountains.
The wind carries sand that cuts the
rocks into strange shapes.

Hot and Cold Deserts

Many deserts get very hot.

The heat plays tricks with the sunlight. The hot ground can look like water, but the water is not real. It is a **mirage**.

The Atacama Desert is
one of the coldest deserts.

Not all deserts are hot. The Atacama Desert
in South America is cold because it is high up
in the mountains.

Days and Nights

The desert sky often has no clouds. Without clouds to block sunlight, the ground gets very hot. Animals must hide from the great heat.

In a desert, there are few places to hide from the sun.

Many animals sleep during the hot day and come out at night.

Deserts get cold at night. There are no clouds to keep in the warmth of the day. Many animals are busy in the cool night.

Rain in the Desert

In some deserts it only rains for a few hours each year. This is enough for some desert plants to grow.

A cactus holds water to use when it is dry.

One of the driest places in the world is the Namib Desert in Africa.

In the driest deserts, it may not rain for many years. This makes it hard for anything to live there.

Desert Storms

Strong winds blow desert sand into the air.
These **dust storms** can last for days.
Smaller winds make swirling **dust devils**
that last for only a few minutes.

This is a dust devil.

These dark clouds show that heavy rain is about to fall.

Rain in the desert comes in heavy storms. They **flood** the land. Heavy rain washes away the sand.

Rivers in the Desert

For most of the year, this river is dry. It needs rain to fill it with water. Without water, you can see the dry bottom. This is called the **river bed**.

a dry river in the desert

When it rains, the river quickly fills with water. It only rains for a short time so the river will only flow for a few hours.

This river will soon be dry again.

The Moving Desert

Desert wind blows the sand into beautiful shapes called **dunes.** Wind carries sand over the crest and drops it on the other side.

The tops of sand dunes are called crests.

These people must shovel the sand from this home.

Wind spreads the desert sand. Sand is
blown across roads and into buildings.

Water in the Desert

Without water, people cannot live in the desert. Water can be found in a few special places.

People walk for days from one water hole to the next.

People in this desert city use water in their homes and gardens. The water comes from under the ground and from a river many miles away.

Phoenix, Arizona, is a big city in the desert.

Desert Map 1

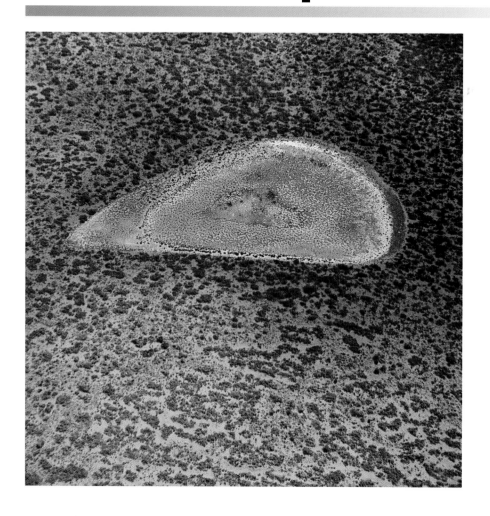

This photo shows part of a sandy desert in Australia. The pear shape is where water was before it was dried up. Salt has been left behind after the water has gone.

This map uses colors to show the same place as the photo. Orange areas show the sandy desert. Gray areas show where the water will be salty. On a map, fresh water is shown as a blue color.

Desert Map 2

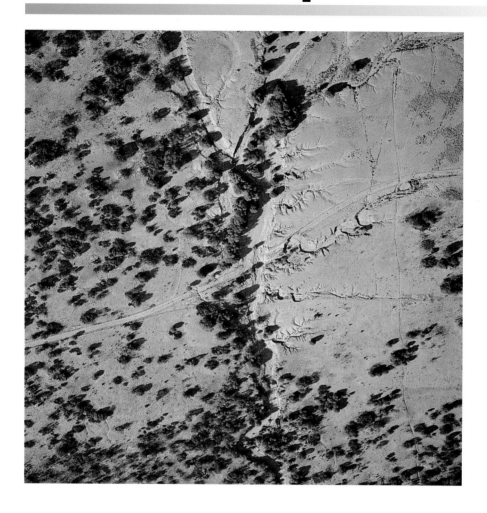

This photo shows a dirt road that crosses the desert in Australia. The road crosses a river. There is no bridge because the river is dry for most of the year.

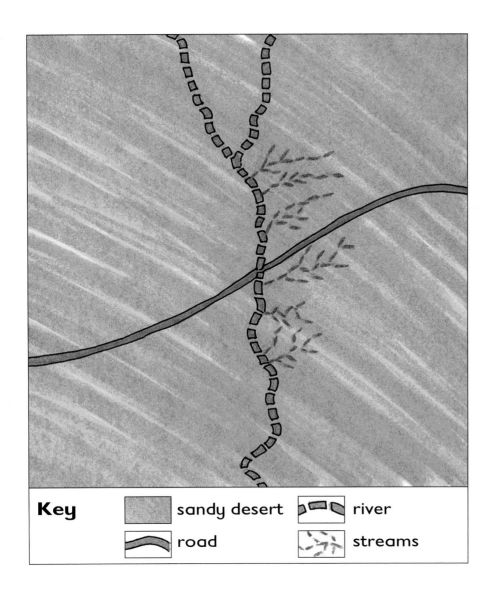

Key

sandy desert	river	
road	streams	

Rivers are shown on maps with blue lines. This river is shown with a broken blue line. This tells us that the river is dry for most of the year.

Desert Map 3

A big rock from space smashed into the desert a long time ago. It made a big hole called a **crater**. People can drive on a road near the crater.

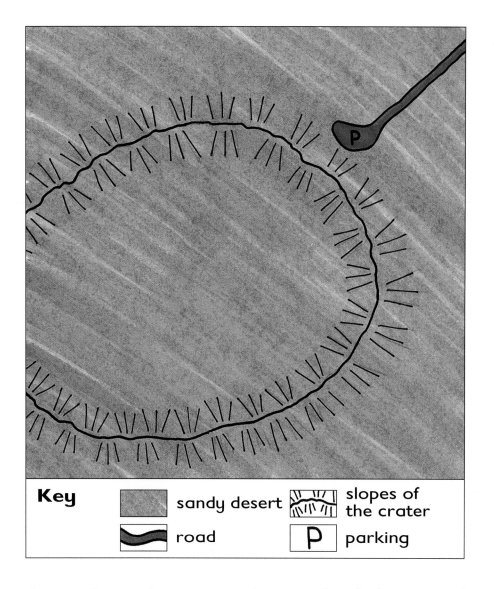

A parking lot is at the end of the road. People can walk up the steep slope of the crater and then down into the middle. The map shows these slopes with thin black lines.

Amazing Desert Facts

The Sahara Desert in Africa is the biggest desert in the world. It is almost as big as the United States.

The biggest dunes in the world are in the Namib Desert in Africa. Sand blown by the wind can strip the paint off a car.

Glossary

crater   large hole formed by an explosion

dunes   hills made out of sand

dust devils   small whirling winds that pick up sand, lasting only a short time

dust storms   strong winds that carry desert sand into the air, often lasting for several days

flood   water from a river that spills onto land

mirage   trick that hot air plays with sunlight, often making roads and sand look like they are covered with water

river bed   bottom of a river

More Books to Read

Bailey, Donna. *Deserts.*
Austin, Tex: Raintree Steck-Vaughn, 1990.

Baylor, Byrd. *The Desert is Theirs.*
New York: Simon & Schuster Childrens, 1975.

Deming, Susan. *The Deserts: A Nature Panarama.*
San Francisco: Chronicle Books. 1991.

Palmer, Joy. *Deserts.*
Austin, Tex: Raintree Steck-Vaughn, 1990.

Reading, Susan. *Desert Plants.*
New York: Facts on File, 1990.

Simon, Seymour. *Deserts.*
New York: Morrow Jr. Books. 1990.

Taylor, Barbara. *Desert Life.*
New York: Dorling Kindersley, 1992.

Index